ECHOES
From The Heart:
Love Throes

Poetry

by

Jeanette Davis

Copyright © 2021 Jeanette Davis

All rights reserved.

ISBN: 978-0-578-35120-9

DEDICATED To

The memory of My mother
Isabella Beverly-Davis-Ashby,
My Aunt Kate Beverly-Green
&

All our elders who guided, and guide us
daily through this maze called LIFE

CONTENTS

Acknowledgements

2-3.	**NOTHING NEW**
4-6.	**ME**
7-8.	**MY EMPTY ROOM**
9.	**WARMTH**
11.	**REINCARNATE**
13.	**ROUND TRIP TICKET**
15.	**PAIN**
16.	**NUCLEUS OF LOVE**
17.	**YOU**
18-19.	**HEART KNOCKS**
21-22.	**AS THE FOG RISES**
23-24.	**MARKING TIME**
25.	**POSSIBILITIES**
26-27.	**INFLUENCES**
28-29.	**FINALLY**
30.	**IGNORANCE**
31-34.	**IT IS WHAT "YOU" SAY IT IS**

35-41.	THE SOUL OF BLACK WOMEN
43-44.	BLACK PERFECTION
45.	TEMPO
46.	YOU ARE MY SECRET
47.	LOVE THROES
48-50.	THE MAIN ATTRACTION
51-53.	LIKE FLOWERS IN FULL BLOOM
55.	WHO SAID THE BLIND CAN'T SEE?
56-57.	FAULTY WIRING
58-59.	BOTTOM LINE
60-61.	"SISTAH"
62-63.	TO THOSE WHO HAVE GIVEN UP
64-65.	ALL ALONE
66-68.	LONG, TALL, LEAN LARRY DEAN
70.	ECHOES
71-74.	YOU ENTERtainED US
75-78.	BABYLON IS FALLING
80-83.	YOU & EYE
86.	Love Fearlessly
98.	About The Author

ACKNOWLEDGMENTS

*All gratitude and thanks to my Creator,
God Almighty, for all blessings, creative abilities,
knowledge, wisdom & overstanding.*

Also

*The two people I have dared to LOVE unconditionally,
and who offered me true unconditional love in return.
One of you were here for a reason
Another for a season, and I await the one true love of a*

LIFETIME

ECHOES
From The Heart:
Love Throes

Poetry

Nothing   New

Between me and you,
there's nothing new
Our hearts are one,
this we always knew

Avoiding each other,
we had things to do
Never letting go
of our inner truth

To meet our goals
we had to be set free
We could not avoid our destinies

So now we're at the sunset of our lives
Time to let this love inside thrive.

You said,

"Start now, when we're old and gray?"

I said,

"Yes my love, we start today"

Echoes From The Heart - Love throes Poetry

You said,

"But Honey, I need plenty lovin'"

I said,

"Baby, snows on the roof, but heat's in the oven.

Love is eternal. It's never through
Love between "US", Baby, is nothing new"

Echoes From The Heart - Love throes Poetry

ME

To Grow To Learn To Love To Feel

To See To Touch

To Give   Too Much

To Want To Have To Want Not

To Be Too Tough To Handle

To Desire To Satisfy

To Hold To Kiss

To Need To Listen

Too Weak To Fight Too Strong To Lose

Too Modest To Gloat

Too Honest To Cheat

Too Afraid   To Sin

Too Human To Behave

Echoes From The Heart - Love throes Poetry

Too Motivated To Give Up

Too Impatient To Wait

To Laugh To Play

Too Serious To Procrastinate.

Too Sensuous To Settle

Too Proud To Beg

Too Black To Betray

Too Curious To Sloth

To Care Too Much

Too Anxious To Please

Too Blessed To Stress

Too Kind Too Loving To Hate

Too Determined To Succeed

Echoes From The Heart - Love throes Poetry

Too Thankful   To Boast

Too Magical   To Fail

My Empty Room

My empty room knows it all.
Its walls my secrets keep
It knows of the countless times
I've called on sleep's release

It knows of secret horrors,
for my soul has seen despair
It knows the times I've cried,
because you weren't there

My empty room has seen it all;
long nights of love denied
It's seen these empty arms of mine
their needs, unsatisfied.

Echoes From The Heart - Love throes Poetry

You ran from me, away from love
and you knew that I was here
You fear my deep sincerity
Wake up, my love, my Dear!

WARMTH

To be together with someone you love

makes life a little less bleak,

solitary
&
Lonesome

To exchange the I for the WE

In the BIGGEST sense of the word,

IT'S COLD OUTSIDE &

Kindness and Affection

Tendered with gentleness

B u i l d s a nice, warm fire inside.

Echoes From The Heart - Love throes Poetry

Love

Is

Patient

REINCARNATE

You whip my soul into submission

You're an old soul
We've met before... Somewhere...

You taunt me with
Your indifference
You've dealt with me before...at Sometime

You know my every
thought and whim

We've realized totality...

Somehow, Sometime, Somewhere
Somehow I know you will soon be gone

Just like before?

Love Is Considerate

Round Trip Ticket

I thought I'd give you a book of the world,

So, you could envision the beauty beyond,

but then I thought, "To see it all in books

and not be there, ain't worth a darn".

So, I finally decided to take you first class,

the way us Capricorns do,

So, dance in the clubs of Cairo my love,

and let Rome fall in love with you

Love

Is

Generous

PAIN

She wooed you with song

You strayed

leaving me all alone

scathed,

deserted...

Yet...
I know...I understand

I'll taste of love

With you

No more

NUCLEUS OF LOVE

You wanted my body

I loved your mind

Your flesh was weak for my embrace

I wanted your soul

You wanted a taste, my love

I wanted the fullness of you

You needed so little

I needed it all

You just didn't know what love is

YOU

We touched...

And all sound gave way to the moment

You smiled...

And the wind hushed...

The earth stilled...Just for a moment

And then you were...

No more

HEART KNOCKS

I said I loved you,
but you did not hear
It wasn't you, my love
The will of others caused the fall

Gift wrapping yourself
for the slaughter by those
who did not care

For those who did not weave
you into their design of life

You willingly gave of yourself for nought

You ignored my suggestion
to slow down.

Echoes From The Heart - Love throes Poetry

It was too much like right

No, it wasn't you, love

How were you to know

what was in their hearts?

You come now with bitterness

and mistrust, wasted years

of not noticing I was there,

and I cared

ARE YOU LISTENING NOW?

Love

Is

Gentle

AS THE FOG RISES

The fog eases as dawn rushes in to reveal
night's mysteries not yet finished
Airy mists of dew tickle earth's bed gently
As thirsty ground is replenished

A daily ritual through time unbroken
as sunrise, tainted by night's disgraces
A lone girl standing at roadside
offering breasts for pay
mind too dulled to choices

Canine eyes see babies tucked behind
cans of trash while still sleeping
Canine ears hear wives and children beaten
by men who've failed and took to drinking

Echoes From The Heart - Love throes Poetry

*When the fog has risen, hearts feel less
guilty of night rage and unseen deeds,
But time will gather all dust into the mist
repaying each by the measure of iniquity*

MARKING TIME

We move through many portals

and corridors, unraveling mysteries

that constantly evade exploration

We search for reasons, answers for things

that amaze and perplex

We strive for excellence, constantly seeing

evidence of rewards in our midst

We make mistakes, regroup, repent,

renege, rectify, and vow not to repeat

We ignore our hearts, our minds remind us

of loved ones lost in time

Echoes From The Heart - Love throes Poetry

We are marking time, searching for purpose

which becomes so clear when love... is

POSSIBILITIES

The more faith you have; the more you

believe; the more goals you set;

the more you achieve

So, reach for the stars pick a mountain to climb

Dare to think big, but give yourself time

Remember no matter

how futile it seems

with faith,

there is NO impossible dream!

INFLUENCES

Everyday people, ejecting unpleasant thoughts, make way for confusion.

VIBRATIONS IN DISCORD ATMOSPHERIC CORROSION OF THE COSMOS *Human body cosmos, untrained mind reacts unconsciously*

PANIC

Controlled atmospheric projections of warmth,

exuding from humanity creates harmony, peace, and comfort.
Thought waves, emotions, physical forces

whether good or evil influence.

The will of man permeates the structure of matter

to achieve its goal. Dreams thereby become reality

Echoes From The Heart - Love throes Poetry

through positive thinking and determination
Think pleasant & Speak Truth
Love, Achieve Good

Finally

*You moved into my heart the day we met
That was a day I'll never forget*

*I was captivated and mesmerized,
You were breathtaking. I was hypnotized.*

*Struck by a thunderbolt, I knew it was love,
the love of my life
but, I had someone else.
the time wasn't right*

*You filled my heart, locked inside,
I could not run; I could not hide
And believe me Baby, I really tried.*

*So many years passed with you still deep within,
and you became my dearest friend*

Echoes From The Heart - Love throes Poetry

The ache was so deep, because I wanted to say,
"I love you Baby in every way"

The farce continued because now you weren't free
I began to wonder, "will we ever be?"

Finally *came the day when you were free,*
And I waited for my heart's release
from lockdown
With only you holding the key

I loved you, but did you love me?

I thought once unlocked,
My heart would be free.
But you kissed me gently saying,

*"**Finally**, it's just you and me."*

IGNORANCE

*Ignorance invades the earth as the air we breathe
Souls in limbo until evolution removes the shackles of
our degradation*

*A brighter day, someday will come to find
many of us wrapped in ignorance' bosom
who are content in our stagnation*

*While the world marches on
to awareness and liberation*

It Is What "YOU" Say It Is

It is what YOU say it is, out of your Mouth
You determine what YOUR life is About
No need to live your life in Doubt
Remove your fears. Remove your Pout
It is what YOU say it is out of YOUR Mouth

YOU say you're weary, your body Tires

YOU say you're broke.
Your bank account Chokes

YOU say you're licked.
Yourself you've Tricked

Say you're Wealthy.
your body is Healthy

Say that you're Fine.
you'll feel Divine

Say you're Strong.
you can't go Wrong

Repeat after me, say, "I am Great"
I don't possess envy; I abhor Hate"
"I am God's child and wonderfully Made

I was born a Sinner,
but now I'm a Winner

Echoes From The Heart - Love throes Poetry

*Saved by His grace; bathed in His Love
I am highly favored and washed in His Blood"*

*It is what I say it is, I dictate my Life
I remove the pitfalls; I remove the Strife*

*I create my future; it's all in MY Mouth
I say and create how My life turns Out*

*God gave me the power to dominate the Earth
This is my birthright given at Birth*

*I say I am Rich, no lack in my Life
My bank account Grows; there is no Strife*

*My family is great; all healthy and Strong
I said it all. We're a happy Throng*

Echoes From The Heart - Love throes Poetry

We were all suffering, God's word set us Free
There is no sorrow, no want or Misery

It is what YOU say it is, out of your Mouth
You determine what YOUR life is About
No need to live your life in Doubt
Remove your fears. Remove your Pout
It is what YOU say it is out of YOUR Mouth

"Life and death are in the power of the tongue:
and they that love it shall eat the fruit thereof"

(Proverbs 18:21).

Echoes From The Heart - Love throes Poetry

THE SOUL OF BLACK WOMEN

When I look in the mirror, I see the eyes of

old and young black women and girl babies

A look of knowing the pain, joy, and strength of just being human

They possess the loins of ancient Candacian Queens battling to assure their existence

Their blackness is in God's image

for the Creator's delight

They are clothed in mysteries

never known to anyone but them

They feel my pain from their own experiences

Above it all, we know each other

Well—it's in the eyes

Echoes From The Heart - Love throes Poetry

My sisters somewhere inside

themselves know the plan

They innately sense when patience

is a strategy and action a must.

Through the eyes in my mirror,

dreams are moving into fruition

Dreams of "doin' what I want to now"

Hathor, the Great Mother of all women am I

I am she who taught the earth

it could give birth

From my deepest sensual being came

Kings and Queens

From my mind, I give strength to a people

Echoes From The Heart - Love throes Poetry

Elevating them from ignorance
to reasonable thought

I have flowered the world with beauty from
the blackest to total loss of melanin

I kissed the Sun with prayers of love, and I birthed
human seed astutely I have been wise in choices until
rape altered the plan

Still, I move stealthily, doing as
I must for the survival of all

These eyes have seen Osiris,
and Horus is a familiar sight

Men seek dark mysteries in my sensuality
They search in primitive places for contemporary
answers while my mind has all they seek

Home to Mother Africa

My heart thrives to the tempo of

the drumbeat

Echoes From The Heart - Love throes Poetry

Back to the inner "knowing"
Back to the promise made long ago
as I kissed her earth upon my uprooting

Back to who I am, why I am and forever will be

Without me, the earth would grow

pale and unfeeling

The rivers would cloud in need of my prayers

The tempestuous soul of "The People"

would lose faith

Without me,

life would be void and without variety

I AM A MUST

When I look in the mirror,
I see the body of Isis
black as coal I stand
The blacker, the silkier to the touch

Echoes From The Heart - Love throes Poetry

My sleekness is as a stallion in the wild
Moving like a lynx, purring when content naturally
loving until pained

There was a time I anointed my body with precious
oils; enjoyed ornaments of gold upon my velvety skin

To touch my skin is to journey into the deepest abyss of
the origin of womanhood

My mirror empowers me with vivid vision of what I
possess, and it tells no lies

It was always there in the mirror
for me to see, and just recently.

I DECIDED TO TAKE A GOOD LOOK!

When I look in the mirror, I see impatience
I see a spirit quickened by its own uniqueness

My body reflects ultimate resentment to unnatural
allegations of inferior being

My mirror shows me knees
unable to bend in the mind

Echoes From The Heart - Love throes Poetry

My tongue is sore from containment
My feet spread wide for the journey are ridiculed

My hair is uniquely mine
They provide tools for its destruction
I will not comply

My full succulent lips are worshipped
They want them too, but pale shall
not have this reward naturally

My cheekbones are proud, structured as
finely chiseled stone, unrelenting and firm

My breasts stand out proudly
expressing their fullness of purpose

My back is strong to bear the burden
My spirituality is who I am

It sculptured my physique for survival
in a desert of ignorance of self

The drum is my heartbeat
Sister Nina told me that

*It's in her eyes too.
The sister who's just like me*

*I still stand tall within the Creator's Bosom
For I came from the first mold of humankind
I am the mother of all*

*The original creation that mankind
wishes he could, but cannot deny
Because only through me,
can mankind validate itself for*

I AM AFRICAN EVE!!!

Love

Is

Affectionate

Echoes From The Heart - Love throes Poetry

BLACK PERFECTION

(Tribute To THE BLACK MAN)

Look at your skin it's as black as coal
Once men and women adorned it with gold

Look at your nose it's spread wide on your face
Look at ancient art to see your rightful place

Look at your hands they belong to you and there's
nothing they haven't and cannot do

Look at your body Black man check it out
You are naturally chiseled
no one else has that clout

Look inside your mind You created all there is
Then HE stole it all, and now says it's his

Look what he's done now that he has it all
It's beginning to crumble it's doomed for a fall

Look at your woman through brand new eyes
She is the treasure. She is the prize

Echoes From The Heart - Love throes Poetry

*Look how he's used her. Our colors are legion
There is a need. There is a reason*

*Look at her skin black velvety smooth
She rebounds from each fall
indestructible she's proved*

*Look at your history
She wore crowns of gold*

*You worshipped her grandeur
Her name was Hathor, we're told*

*Look towards Nubia to find what went wrong
Find out the truth about where you belong*

*Look around you and it'll be made clear,
that you are the father of all that is here*

*Look inside your soul
where God makes His home,
and you'll understand where I'm coming from*

*Look at Perfection that's what you're all about
Don't take it from me, go ahead check it out!*

Echoes From The Heart - Love throes Poetry

TEMPO

Moving in continuity, energies personified,

Youth races on, STACCATO

Phew! Lucky to reach Middle-age,

Pianissimo

Old Age awaits the GRAND FINALE

All movement reaches Crescendo

It is done
How quickly the end comes
That's life
The joy, the tears, the sorrows
The unsure tomorrows

Youth will not listen; the aged know it all
People surviving behind self-made walls

Afraid to touch, terrified to feel
Refusing their humanity, a chance to be real

YOU ARE MY SECRET, shhh

*A sensitive warm human being you are
I know, I've touched your soul
Words were said, feelings were hurt
now your heart for me runs cold*

*If you could have seen my heart cry out
in utter pain and despair,
Then maybe you would have understood
my need to have you near*

*A fragile, passionate creature you are
I know, I've basked in your warmth
I let you go free. My biggest regret
My memories you'll always haunt*

Love Throes

Oh, fiery passion my soul release
from unfamiliar fantasy
You punish my body torment my mind.
Distorting my view of the upward climb

Animal passion you strike at will
Weakening my flesh, overpowering my will
You haunt my mind, fill my body with lust
longing for someone I fear to trust

Oh, bodily greed, temptation's caprice
I bargain for my sanity
Release my Being from your arduous hold,
Release your bind, spare my soul.

The "MAIN" Attraction

*I was born into it. It clings to me.
I've gotten used to it although at times, it's uncomfortable*

*I feel it, cleanse it, nurture it, clothe it
and adjusted to it in time.*

*Others see it, but I don't,
when looking at them.*

*I know it's there because I can feel, touch,
taste, smell and see it whenever I choose to.*

*I pamper it, and use it continuously
because I can't get away from it.
It lets me know when it is neglected,*

*It is happy when fulfilled
It's an additive that I need,*

*and must have. I can master it
to its highest potential,
or let it fester into uselessness*

*I thought it belonged to me,
but recently I've found it does not
I can only use it until it wears out*

*Only one can fit me perfectly,
I can arrange it anyway it will bend
I have stretched it, slimmed it,*

*enhanced it, and sometimes shared it
It always does what I want it to do
Sometimes to my chagrin
I deal with it because I have no choice*

*Well, I do, but the options are few
I live in it to exist in the world,*

but it is not the Main Attraction

Echoes From The Heart - Love throes Poetry

*It is my Earth Suit. It is not I.
The real ME no one can see, is inside.*

Inside of me is the essence that is eternal

***I AM SPIRIT
I AM THE MAIN ATTRACTION***

*Don't let my appearance distract
you from the real me.*

*Anyone can dress to other's
satisfaction, deceive you, mesmerize you,*

*and tempt you when they are in the flesh
So
Don't get distracted from the real me.*

*Take a close look inside
I may live in the flesh,
But*

I WALK IN THE SPIRIT!

Echoes From The Heart - Love throes Poetry

Like Flowers In Full Bloom

Your eyes shine so brightly, they're so wise

They've seen so much...
The lines of time surround them
on a face that's soft to the touch

You are the seniors... The wise ones of our time

We pay you homage

because you're so gen-u-ine

You are the older ones among us,
who are flowers in full bloom.
You've reaped harvests,
that the young have yet to sow
Life has given you the clues
You've all paid your dues.

and we love you so

Echoes From The Heart - Love throes Poetry

*You look at us so lovingly
as you guide us through the maze
The understanding nods you give,
you've seen these kinds of days*

You are the seniors... The wise ones of our time

We pay you homage

because you're so gen-u-ine

*You are the older ones among us,
who are flowers in full bloom.
You've reaped harvests,
that the young have yet to sow
Life has given you the clues
You've all paid your dues.*

and we love you so

*For a flower to be created,
a seed must first be planted.*

Echoes From The Heart - Love throes Poetry

The same is true for us.
That's nature's way
The flower has a life span.
It grows according to plan.
It matures into full bloom, in full array

We are all like flowers
in different stages of its growth
By the time we reach full bloom
we would have seen much on this earth

You are the seniors... The wise ones of our time

We pay you homage

because you're so gen-u-ine

You are the older ones among us,
who are flowers in full bloom.
You've reaped harvests,
that the young have yet to sow
Life has given you the clues
You've all paid your dues.

and we love you so

Love

Is

Nurturing

Who Said the Blind Can't See?

With sightless eyes, they gyrate among us
viewing the souls of others

Never an ugly face do they see
in their world of fleeting vibrations

They feel with their being,
sifting for the inner sanctum of man

They are gifted to behold that which
we painfully seek to be revealed

How shameful of us to have eyes
and see not

the BEAUTY beyond the shell

Echoes From The Heart - Love throes Poetry

FAULTY WIRING

"Well," I thought,
"It doesn't pay to think these days"
Just when I thought I had a good grasp on things
everything fell apart

Mechanized minds cancel out humane qualities

Everything is computerized. Man wants robots

He's so sorry we're not mechanized,

but he's working on it

Remember when we were kids,
all the dos and don'ts?
We believed in them and adhered

Echoes From The Heart - Love throes Poetry

*Programmed, destined to carry out
other's will and directions.*

Where did I lose me?

*Did I really know me at all,
or is this flesh and blood just a pretense?*

*Is it an illusion, to make me believe
I'm not a machine?*

*If so, why do I want to feel, to love, to touch?
I want to; but they call it neuroses,
and everyone knows that's bad
especially during a pandemic*

So, I drift... in their reality hoping evolution

will repeat the beginning so I can find me

and be human again

BOTTOM LINE (Cocaine Addicts)

They plunge into the bowels of Hell seeking fulfillment searching aimlessly, they stumble on,

mesmerized by the illusion of beauty, they're pulled deeper and deeper into an abyss of despair and desperation

The need to have, to taste, to feel, to see to sample all there is...means nothing

The veil of illusion disrobes before them

revealing its hideous deceit

*Tortured souls reach out to them from below vying to pull them deeper
There is but one way out*

Echoes From The Heart - Love throes Poetry

They seemed to have not come far...
yet while gazing upward
they see many struggling to escape
to the light that is unseen, but surely there

The climb is arduous, endless
and without gratification

They thirst. They hunger. They cry out
for aid, for mercy...no one hears

They finally realize, it's a lonely
journey and the raging fires of Hell
are not around them, nor beneath.

IT'S WITHIN!

"Sistah"

You are beauty, black velvet
in your grace and regal splendor
You love thoroughly You give totally.
You get so little, but you win...sometimes

You are simply gorgeous, Queen of the Nile
in sensuous skin of velvet

Mysterious and of cool demeanor

You seek love
You need love

You get love...sometimes

You are my strength ebony lady
Inside are dreams and determination

Echoes From The Heart - Love throes Poetry

You wisely strive
You are alone
You are undefeated...in time

You are God's treat
My precious sister

Encased in love and understanding

You give me hope
You give me joy
I offer my love & support for all time

To Those Who Have Given Up

Oh, Ye of little faith
Dipped into the "sea of ignorance'

You run away from self
Ye who are closest to God than all others,
who are imitators asleep

Awaken YOU of luscious full lips
and hair so rare that twinkles in sunlight

Ye who are emulated
Now emulate your mockers
bringing you home to you

Rem Sleep has sedated your soul

Wearing blue eyes to hide self, exposes your plot
They are laughing at you

*We twinge in pain because you've
given up on being one of us.*

*Ye of little faith
you have tired of the fight*

*You are ready to be absorbed
The mind goes first, you know*

*By flaunting self-hate,
You show they can win*

All Alone

*When you see me, you categorize
because you've been told,
"You'll get hurt and left without love"
So, you isolate your soul*

*"Your sensitivities trod upon, the games
and untruths are cold"
So, you build yourself
a fortress to isolate your soul*

*Each time betrayal comes,
cards of hope for man starts to fold.
The only way it seems you'll get
through is to isolate your soul*

Echoes From The Heart - Love throes Poetry

No one may enter through these walls.
Experience has sealed all holes

You long for the touch of a
warm human being
to love, to have, to hold

To pierce through the fortress
of loneliness and isolation of your soul

Echoes From The Heart - Love throes Poetry

Long, Tall, Lean Larry Dean

*(A Posthumous Tribute to a Great Instructor
at Morgan State University, & Wonderful Human Being)*

*His smile touched our hearts
as his words calmed our fears
All of us who knew him shed many tears*

*His strategy was love
His direction was sure
He cared for us all who knocked on his door*

*"You can do it." He said
"I know you can"
When we lost Larry,
we lost a wonderful man*

*I smile when I think of his joking ways
How he made us laugh on those dreary days
He was kind and sweet in a gentle way
We missed him dearly on the radio at WEAA*

Echoes From The Heart - Love throes Poetry

He guided the pros. You know who you are
Had he not touched your life
Would you be a star?

He was "Big Daddy Dean" to the younger crew
He gave them someone to look up to

Larry would want us to help the youth
Give them direction; lead them to truth
To give of ourselves in a positive way
To remember that ego must not bar the way

We love you too, Greer You stood by his side
You were his love, his joy, his bride
When HE needed someone,
you were always there
with a ready smile and full of cheer

Echoes From The Heart - Love throes Poetry

**When doubting myself, I can still hear Larry say,
"I know you can do it, you're made that way"**

Love

Is

Compassion

Echoes From The Heart - Love throes Poetry

ECHOES

We Wished

We Wanted

We Missed

We're Haunted

with memories of what could have been

Echoes From The Heart - Love throes Poetry

"YOU ENTERtainED US

(Excerpt from my book: "Black Survival in White America:

From Past History to the Next Century")

GOD has not forgotten us
When He smiled upon us,

Maya Angelou came forth,

majestic, regal, and dignified

tripping words off of tongue

as if birthing them anew

Nikki entered.

fiery, yet poetically gently reminding,
scolding and lovingly soothing the soul
of black folk into action

Echoes From The Heart - Love throes Poetry

What of Langston's arrival?
Can't you hear him pounding out verse to drum,
pushing deferred dreams into fruition?

When jazzy Bird arose
Mr. Cool was on the scene
transcending and soaring
our spirits to unlimited heights

Mahalia appeared.
She "sang" for us about joy, love
and heavenly praise

Nat was God sent,
He was the King
With his velvety voice enchanting us
with "Unforgettable" melodies of love

Echoes From The Heart - Love throes Poetry

And how about Bessie.
singing those low-down funky blues?

And, hey, the "A" train didn't leave the station
until Duke got there

Can you hear the voice of an angel? That's Marian
enthralling the world with her
"Once in a hundred year's voice"

And Satchmo, he cooked with that horn,

&

didn't Handy groove,
while Bojangles moved to the "tap dance" beat?

Zora Neale knew we were a "cracked plate",
And Countee Cullen came to set us straight

Echoes From The Heart - Love throes Poetry

Who can forget Nina with her "Heartbeat",
& Lorraine's "Raisin" had us on our feet

Mom's Mabley made us laugh
through our tears,
and when we were sad,
Pigmeat and Skillet were here

And how about Pryor, satire, and all,
and then came Murphy he's having a ball

God gave us Aretha to caress our souls,
Carmen McRae? She broke the mold

There's no one like Black Folk with spirits so sweet,

and we can "Jerusalema" to Mother Africa's beat

(I hear you Master KG & Nomcebo)

Echoes From The Heart - Love throes Poetry

BABYLON IS F
A
L
L
I
N
G

Black American brothers and sisters, WAKE UP! White
Babylon's falling down round' you
You'll never get what they've got
Before you do, they will see you rot, in their

jails

Don't be fooled by their ploys

Echoes From The Heart - Love throes Poetry

REMOVE YOUR BLINDING VEILS!

BLACK American brothers and sisters,

WAKE UP!

You've cried for four hundred plus years

You sleep the sleep of a drunken man,

living in the house of a brutal Klan

Their souls are consumed with greed
Don't be deluded, you're not included,
YOU'VE OUTLIVED THEIR NEED!

They stole your legacy from Mother Africa,
and the Black Madonna is crying
Their system is anathema
Your struggle for freedom is dying

Echoes From The Heart - Love throes Poetry

***Black American brothers and sisters WAKE UP!
They're stealing your culture from you***

*Your future looks very grim.
You're losing your Melanin
You're beginning to act just like them*

Don't be fooled and absorbed

*They stole your legacy from Mother Africa,
and the Black Madonna is crying
Their system is anathema
Your struggle for freedom is dying*

*The world is looking to you
to see what you will do*

*You're in the house of a greedy man
Are you too close to see and understand?*

Echoes From The Heart - Love throes Poetry

Black greatness has never been equaled
We're overdue for a sequel

Find out who you are
YOURS IS THE BRIGHTEST STAR!

They stole your legacy from Mother Africa,
and the Black Madonna is crying
Their system is anathema
Your struggle for freedom is dying

AMERICAN BROTHERS & SISTERS WAKE UP!

(Written soon after the death of Dr. Martin Luther King, Jr.) by
Jeanette Davis © 1968

Love

Is

Hugs & Kisses

YOU & EYE

I am your cool breeze on a hot summer's day
I am the love you're seeking that won't fade or stray

I am forever yours till my dying day
Even death won't keep my love away

I am eternal spirit bound to yours always
I am the love you're seeking that will forever stay

I am your joy when sadness pierces your day
I am the peace within you, a golden ray

I am the one who makes you smile, just think of me
I am the muse in your life. You are my destiny

I am the solid rock upon which you stand
I am the voice that tells you that you "can"

Echoes From The Heart - Love throes Poetry

I am the one you seek who knows who you are
I am the one who knows you are the brightest star

I am the one you've sought after for a lifetime
I am the one you found at just the right time

I am your greatest love, the one you seek
I am right here in front of you, look at me

I am the love you seek. God made me for you
I am the flame sent to ignite the fire in you

I am the one who fell for your loving charms
I am the one you need to hold in your arms

I am the sun, the stars, the moon, and the sky
YOU are the apple of my eye

I am the warmth on a cold Winter's eve
I am the sweet love air that you breathe

I am the tempo of the music inside of you too
I am the heartbeat that dwells inside of you

Echoes From The Heart - Love throes Poetry

I am the tender lover that you seek
I know who you are; do you know me?

You are the rhythm of time: Its essence, its pace
You are universal love: It's in your face

You are God's favorite. God flows through you
You are God's gift to life. You are love's truth

You are gentle, trusting, kind and aware
You are beautiful, fiery, & fierce beyond compare

You are flowers in Springtime, lavender and sweet
You are Fall's lovely colors before trees fall asleep

You are a golden-toned beauty, with purity of soul
Even inside of you is a heart of gold

You are the misty morning dew falling gently
to earth
You emitted harmony and serenity on the day of
your birth

Echoes From The Heart - Love throes Poetry

You spread beauty and nurture everything anew
You sprinkle it everywhere, like morning dew

You're a great treasure the world has yet to adore
But I see you and love you ever more

You were right here, for everyone to see
God made sure I saw your rare quality

You are priceless; this I quickly sensed
In life there is no coincidence

You are a rare jewel created just for me
That's why I can see you so clearly

You are worthy of a great love in your life
You are God's CHOSEN one, God's Delight

You're not forgotten. It took a lifetime for you to see
You are gifted true love. You are gifted me

Love

Is

Faithfulness

Love

Is

Compassion

Echoes From The Heart - Love throes Poetry

Love Fearlessly

For Those who dare to Love without fear
Knowing,
We do not choose when we Love,
or who we Love
Love chooses both
For Cupid's arrow is swift and sure
To strike whom the Gods choose for us
There are no accidents or coincidences
That is why we call it falling in Love
We are defenseless
Enjoy every moment of Love's Bliss
when it is True Love
True Love that bonds the mind,
emotions, spirit, and body
that is the true Love we should seek

Love

Is

Truthfulness

Love

Is

Goodness

Love

Is

You

&

Me

Love

Is

Harmony

Love

Is

Kind

Love

Is

Caring

Love

Is

Sharing

Love

Is

Unconditional

Love

Is

Forgiving

Love

Is

Long Suffering

Echoes From The Heart - Love throes Poetry

Echoes From The Heart - Love throes Poetry

About The Author

I received my Bachelor of Science Degree in Broadcast Journalism, and graduated Summa Cum Laude from Morgan State University.

I am an honorably discharged veteran of the U.S. Army.

My play, "Grandma Loved Roses", won Baltimore's WMAR-TV's (channel 2) Drama Competition for Black Writers, and was televised in 1985.

I have appeared on "Geraldo", "Rolonda", and various other television and radio talk shows for promotion of my book **"Black Survival in White America: From Past History to the Next Century"**. *(This book" can only be obtained from me, the author- see email below).*

Published books on Amazon.com by Jeanette Davis:

"The Great Divide Between Blacks & Whites"

"Black, Just Like My Mama" (Autobiography)

"Soulful Journey: The Business of Beings"

"Echoes From the Heart: Love Throes Poetry"

"Master Being Human" (to be released January 2022)

Email: jayadds80@gmail.com

Echoes From The Heart - Love throes Poetry

Echoes From The Heart - Love throes Poetry

www.ingramcontent.com/pod-product-compliance
Lightning Source LLC
Chambersburg PA
CBHW071144090426
42736CB00012B/2215